T0018280

THE ESSENTIAL BOOK OF
SPELLS

Elements

THE ESSENTIAL BOOK OF
SPELLS

—

Magic to enchant
your world

MARIE BRUCE

SIRIUS

SIRIUS

This edition published in 2023 by Sirius Publishing, a division of
Arcturus Publishing Limited,
26/27 Bickels Yard, 151–153 Bermondsey Street,
London SE1 3HA

ISBN: 978-1-3988-2612-0
AD008693UK

Printed in China

Contents

Introduction

SIT FOR A SPELL

Spell books have been around for centuries and, whether handmade or traditionally published, most witches worth their salt have at least one volume of spells that they reach for in times of crisis. In Wiccan circles, this spell-book is known as the Book of Shadows, or BOS. In other circles, it is called a grimoire. Whatever its name, the spell book is a vital tool for magical practitioners, providing information, instruction, comfort and a sense of control when life gets messy.

Often, personal spell-books are burnt after the practitioner's death, but there are still a few around if you know where to look. The Witchcraft Museum in Cornwall has a collection, which is worth a visit if you are curious. Many witches and practitioners like to create their own spell-books, writing out their tried-and-trusted spells and rituals in a private journal.

It should also be said that other witches prefer to work entirely from published books of spells, such as this one. These books can be a great time-saving device, as they tend to hold spells for all purposes and are easy to use. Of course, spells can always be adapted, or used to inspire the practitioner to write their own original spells, so there is more than one way to utilize a book like this one.

In this book, I have drawn together spells, rituals, visualizations and blessings to suit a variety of situations and circumstances. My intention is that this book will become a trusted resource—one you can reach for whenever you feel you need a little magical assistance to make your life run more smoothly. All the spells utilize easily sourced ingredients and the standard tools of magic (see pages 38-41).

This book is for all those people who are tired of being buffeted by life and who want to steer their own course. It is for people who are fed up with feeling powerless and want to feel powerful instead. It is for those individuals who are looking for a life-enhancing way to develop personal autonomy, achieve goals, and bring about a harmonious and successful life.

This, then, is my gift to you: a Book of Shadows with which you can navigate the ups and downs of life. So pour yourself a nice brew and sit for a spell as we dive into the fascinating world of witchery and spellcraft. Your magical journey is about to begin.

Blessed be,
Marie Bruce

CHAPTER ONE

Secrets of Sorcery

The image of a witch poring over a huge tome of spells is an iconic one in popular culture and it's not that far from the truth. Most witches do keep spell-books on hand and they study their craft voraciously. However, today's witches are a far cry from the repulsive hags of the stereotype. Witchcraft is actually a gentle practice, which honours nature and respects all forms of life. It is a spirituality that celebrates the seasons, freedom of spirit, equality, diversity and tolerance.

Spell-casting is an art form and an intrinsic part of witchery. It takes time to learn but, as with any other craft, practice makes perfect. Given time, you will be able to whip up a spell in a few moments, once you have learnt how magical correspondences (or tools used in spell-craft) work and which phases of the moon are best for which types of magic.

To begin with though, we all had to learn the basics. Magic is something that requires serious commitment and attention to detail. It must be approached with respect and a certain amount of reverence, for you are tapping into universal energies of great power and potential.

What Is a Spell?

A spell or magic ritual is the ability to cast an influence over the events of one's life, using willpower and the powers of the natural world combined. It is a technique used by witches to facilitate a specific outcome, or to bring into being the desire of the witch. Spells are not evil and magic is neither black nor white. It is simply energy that is directed towards an intention. Whether that intention is for good or ill is down to the individual witch, but the power of spell-craft itself is always neutral.

I have often described spell-casting as "prayer with props". Witches are working with the powers of the universe to attract their desired outcome. We use tools such as candles, incense, incantations, written intentions, crystals, plants and so on, to help us maintain our focus and to bring in aspects of the natural energies with which we work.

Spell-casting is a collaboration between you and the universe, and you have to practise in alignment with the universal tides in order to cast an effective spell or ritual. Most spells, but not all, incorporate some kind of incantation — that is a series of words that are spoken out loud. Sometimes the incantation takes the form of a repetitive chant or a song. Its purpose is to state the intention of the spell.

HOW DO SPELLS WORK?

Spells work by attracting your intention towards you, using the magnetic fields of the universe. Think of the universe as a huge mirror that is designed to reflect your intentions back at you, like for like. This means that what you focus on is what you get. Keeping your thoughts positive will bring good things into your life, while allowing your thoughts to become negative will attract more things for you to complain about!

To make positive and effective magic, it is important to have a clear intention and a positive attitude towards the outcome. You must expect good things to come to you, and in a good way. This keeps your personal vibration on a high frequency, which results in positive manifestation of your intentions. Having doubts that your magic will work, or being very sceptical about magic in general, can delay the outcome, or even sabotage it completely.

BACK UP YOUR SPELLS

You must always be prepared to back up your spells in the mundane world. You can't expect magic to do all the work for you. Witches are not passive or apathetic, they are active participants in their own lives, which means that for every spell they cast, they will take action in the real world to help the magic to manifest.

What does this mean in practice? It means that if you are casting spells for financial freedom, you will need to stop racking up debts. It means that if you cast for a new job, you need to apply for positions and brush up your interview technique, and if you are casting for love, then you need to be open to meeting new people.

Every time you cast a spell, ask yourself how you are going to support the magic in the mundane world. Do you need to make a phone call, send an email or apply for a new post, stop spending on frivolous things, join a club, book a trip? What can you do that will show the universe that you are serious about your goal and that you are willing to put yourself out there along with your magic?

WHY DO WITCHES CAST SPELLS?

Magic is far from new. It has been around for centuries, though we might not always recognize it as such. Many of the things we take for granted and have an understanding of today, such as modern medicine or the laws of chemistry for instance, would have been viewed as feats of magic or alchemy in the past. We only need to think of technology to see how fast our world is changing, growing and developing. So the things that people once viewed as magic are now a part of our everyday lives.

Why do witches cast spells? Well, there are lots of reasons, but the main one is that it gives us a sense of personal power and control over our lives. It is also a way to help others. It can be a great comfort to light a candle and say a few words when a loved one is ill and you are feeling helpless. It can be a healing experience to mix up a bath potion to use after a long day at work, or a great relief to hear the cat meowing at the door shortly after you have cast a safe-return spell.

To put it in the simplest of terms, casting spells can make you feel better. It makes you feel as if you done something to address whatever situation you find yourself in — and you have! Spell-casting is a powerful technique, one which even the more orthodox religions use, though they would never refer to it as magic. Have you ever gone into a church and been invited to light a candle for someone who is struggling? This is spell-craft known by another name — prayer. Essentially it is all one and the same thing, and that is asking for help from a greater power.

Becoming adept at spells and rituals means that you need never feel helpless again, because there is always something you can do. Even in the worst of times, such as bereavement, you can cast for strength and healing to help with the grieving process. There is nothing that cannot be improved with a little sprinkling of magic — no sticky situation that cannot benefit from a spell to smooth it out.

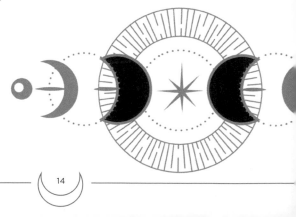

Can Spells Go Wrong?

S ometimes a spell might not work very well, or it might not work in the way that you envisaged it would. Often this is simply a case of rewording and tweaking the original spell. For magic to be effective, you need to be very clear and specific as to what you are casting for. As an example, if you cast a spell to bring a new companion into your life, then you might find that you manifest a new pet rather than a new lover! If it is a lover you want, that is what your spell should focus on.

Being specific is the key to a successful spell. Focus on exactly what you want. Don't leave it open to interpretation, because the universe doesn't understand nuance or vague suggestions. Be clear, be specific and be bold. Magic will usually manifest *something,* so clarity is essential. It is rare that a spell has no effect whatsoever, because you are sending energy out into the universe and that energy has to transform and come back to you in some way.

If you think that your spell simply hasn't worked, then check that all your correspondences were in alignment with one another and with your goal. If they are, then you can always recast the spell. Some big goals need spells to be repeated over time to bring about manifestation. If the spells still don't seem to be working, it could be that what you are asking for isn't for your highest good. If this is the case, then another path will be offered to you instead, one that suits you much better, so don't lose heart. The universe really *is* on your side.

How To Manage the Power of Magic

E veryone holds a spark of magic within them, a personal source of power that they can use to manifest their goals and ambitions. When you cast a spell, you are weaving together your own personal power with the greater power of the universe or nature. These two powers combined create magic and manifestation. This magical power is a form of energy, so it can never be diminished – it simply changes shape and form. You send energy out into the world when you cast a spell and that energy changes form, returning to you as the manifestation of your goal. This is why your spells should be cast with a positive mind-set, to bring back positive results.

Some spells take more energy than others. A spell to manifest a new house would take significantly more power than a spell to bring about a quiet day at work. This is why large goals require repeated spells, because they need more energy. Likewise, several people working together in a coven can do more with one spell than a solitary practitioner can, again because there is more energy involved.

Managing energy is all part of being a witch or magical practitioner. As you cast a spell you will feel the energy and excitement build, until the spell is released in some way. This could mean burning, burying or scattering spell ingredients, to release the power of the magic. Building energy is an intrinsic aspect of spell-casting and it has its own guidelines, known as the Law of the Power, which is:

1   To Know
2   To Dare
3   To Will
4   To Be Silent

What this essentially means is that you must know what type of spell you are going to cast and for what purpose. You must then have the courage to cast the spell and will it into being. The final rule can be the hardest to follow for some people, because you must remain completely silent about what you have done.

Witches do not discuss the spells they are casting until manifestation has occurred. The reason for this is that talking about the spell is thought to reduce the power and the possibility of it working. Have you ever told someone of an exciting new opportunity or romance, only to have the whole thing fall through, as if you had somehow jinxed the outcome? Don't diminish the power of the spell by gossiping about it. After all, it is no one else's business what you get up to with a candle! Magic works best in secret, so maintain the Law of the Power. We will be looking at the ethics of magic in the next chapter, but for now ensure that you work with good intentions and you won't go far wrong.

It's Not a Black and White Issue

True magic is pure energy. It is neither black nor white, good nor bad. Although some people might describe themselves as white or black witches, this is really just to let others know where their intentions lie. A white, or good, witch would be someone who casts spells to help others, while the black, or bad, witch would cast with a harmful intent, such as spells for revenge. There are also racial connotations here which cannot be ignored and for that reason, many modern practitioners are steering clear of terms like black and white magic.

It is the intention of the practitioner which determines whether a spell is cast for good or ill. Magic has often been likened to electricity, which can be used to power life-saving hospital equipment or the electric chair, depending on how it is directed. The same is true of magical power – it can be used to heal or to harm, depending on how the practitioner directs it, but it is essentially a neutral energy.

Types of Magic and Spells

There are many different kinds of magic, and different witches prefer different spells. Some like to work with candles, others prefer to use living plants in the garden. Hedge Witches work predominantly with herbs, Kitchen Witches with potions and food spells, Green Witches with the earth and the forest, and Scribe Witches with runes, sigils (magic symbols) and the written word. It must be said, however, that most witches work with most types of magic, we just have our preferences for certain tools and spells.

CHAPTER TWO

Power Play

Y ou have the potential to blaze a path of magic right through your life, using spell-craft to influence your choices, decisions and dilemmas. You can use the craft of magic to attract the right kind of people to you and to open doors to the right places and opportunities. Before you do any of this, however, you need to understand your obligations as a practitioner of magic.

Like any other kind of power and authority, magic comes with the weight of responsibility. It will give you autonomy over your own life, but you must ensure that your magic doesn't interfere with the lives of other people. Therefore, there are certain guidelines that you should follow in order to get the most from your spells, whilst also safeguarding the free will of others.

Ethics of Magic

Before you cast any kind of ritual or spell, you should ask yourself if it will have an impact on anyone other than yourself. Witches do not cast spells on other people, but we do weave a web of magic around ourselves in order to attract the things we want. What does this mean in practice? Well, it means that you should never cast spells for another person without their permission. This includes magic for healing the sick and helping someone who is dealing with addiction. It can be difficult watching someone you care about struggle, but unless you have permission to cast spells for them, try to help in more mundane ways instead.

There is a good reason for this and it is all about free will. In casting spells without permission, you are effectively tampering with someone's free will. You could also be preventing them from learning a spiritual or life lesson with your interference. By all means have a chat with them and test the ground to see how they feel about magic, but unless you have permission to work spells on their behalf, stick to casting only for yourself. While this might seem selfish, it is really the most ethical option. If someone you love is sick, but you know they wouldn't like the idea of magic, then instead of casting healing spells for them, cast spells for strength and service around yourself, so that you can be there when they need you, and so that you are more inspired to help in a way that they find most comforting.

Another example would be that of love spells. You should only cast spells upon yourself in order to attract more love into your life. Love cannot be forced, even by magic. It is a gift that must be offered freely, without conditions attached. So, if you want more romance in your life, cast a spell to attract more romantic situations towards you, rather than one to turn your partner into Casanova! Always bear in mind the ripple effect of any spells you cast and try to ensure that they do not encroach on the free will of anyone else.

THE THREEFOLD LAW

One of the reasons witches are such sticklers for protecting free will is because of the Threefold Law, which states that whatever you send out magically will come back to you with three times the force and three times the consequences. This is why you should never cast in the spirit of envy, vengeance or spite, because, essentially, you are only hurting yourself in the long run, when all those emotions are directed back at you in some way.

The Threefold Law means that whatever you send out will come back to you, so if you are sending out positive, happy vibrations, you will receive positive and happy opportunities in return. In Wiccan belief we often refer to the Threefold Law as the Harm None rule, which simply states: "An it harm none, do what you will." This little mantra reminds us to keep our thoughts, words, deeds and magic positive in nature, so that we are not inadvertently encroaching on someone's free will, or causing harm to another living creature. It is a very life-enhancing law to live by, for it means that we are always mindful of how our actions might impact other people, animals and the natural world around us.

Emotions and Intention

Your emotions are the fuel to your spells. How you are feeling when you cast a spell can have an impact on how well it works. Likewise, so can your state of health. Generally speaking, the more positive and upbeat you are when you cast a spell, the better it will work. If emotion is the fuel for your magic, then intention is the vehicle in which it travels. You need both to cast an effective spell, otherwise, like a car without petrol or petrol without a car, the magic is going nowhere. Where many neophyte witches fall down, however, is to assume that you state your intention once and the job is done. It isn't quite that simple.

Intention is all about mind-set, belief and behaviour. You can state the intention that you will find love, but unless you also *believe* that you are loveable and *act* from a loving heart, the intention falls flat. This is because your actions and behaviours are not in alignment with your magical goal. In short, you are not backing up your spell with complementary actions that support your intention.

To set a true intention, you must first of all believe that it is possible for you to have what you are casting for. You must know deep in your heart that you deserve to have it. You must act as if it is already coming to you and feel a sense of certainty that you will have it. Finally, you must prepare to receive it by making space for it in your life. This process is the same regardless of the goal. If setting an intention were as simple as just writing it down on a piece of paper, then we would all be manifesting our heart's desires all the time! Writing down your intentions does help, especially if you can see it every day, as this will help to keep you on track with regards to your mind-set, but it is really just a visual cue to set the intention internally, within your heart, mind and soul. Only when you are living and breathing your intention on a daily basis will the manifestation of your spell occur, because you are giving the universe a full picture of what you want it to reflect back at you. To put it in the simplest terms:

Emotion + Intention = Magical Manifestation

Timing

When you perform your magic will have an effect on how well it works. While emergency spells can and should be cast as and when the crisis occurs, for all spells that are planned in advance, you will need to ensure that you are casting them at the right time. All the spells in this book clearly state when they should be cast, but once you begin to create your own spells and rituals, you will need to have a working knowledge of magical timing and how it works.

THE LUNAR CYCLE

Magic is created in accordance with the phases of the moon. This is the most important aspect of magical timing, because the magnetic pull of the moon works with the universal tides to either pull something towards you or take it away. That being the case, your spells to manifest something should be cast during the period from new to full moon, whereas spells that banish something should be cast from full to waning moon.

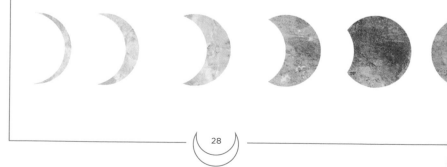

New Moon

This is the beginning of the lunar cycle, although the moon cannot actually be seen in the sky until a few days after the new moon. For this reason, the start of the new moon phase is sometimes known as dark moon and is typically a time of rest. As soon as the first sliver of light appears — a delicate crescent moon that looks like a backwards C — it is time to start thinking about what you want the next lunar cycle to bring you. The new moon is a time for sowing seeds of new projects, weighing up the pros and cons of a situation and assessing the need for a change. Remember that all seeds are sown in darkness to grow with the light. Now is the time to decide what you want.

Waxing Crescent

The light increases as the crescent moon fills leftwards. This is the time when you set your mind on exactly what it is you want. You don't need to know how you will achieve the goal, just set your intention and allow the universe to work out the details for you.

First Quarter Moon

In this phase, the moon looks as if it has been cut in half — half of it is illuminated by the sun, the other remains in darkness. Now is the time to take action, so brush up your CV or start applying for jobs if a career change is your goal. Make a positive start on a new project. Get out more and meet new people if you want to draw friends to you. Make a start on your goal, even if only in a small way.

Waxing Gibbous

The moon now appears to be three-quarters full. Now is the time for action – it's not enough to have a goal; you need to work towards it. The lunar energies won't do it all for you! It is a collaboration and you need to put the effort in too. At this time, the energies are growing stronger and magnetically pulling in your intention, so help it along with positive action.

Full Moon

The full moon lights up the night sky and her effect can be felt by everyone. This is a time of abundance, of goals coming to fruition and labouring on long-term ambitions. The full moon offers a boost if you are flagging, lending much needed energy to your goal. The powers of the full moon can be felt for three nights in a row – the night before, the night of, and the night after the moon is full. This is also the most powerful time for all kinds of magic, divination and spell-casting, so don't waste it!

Waning Gibbous

As the moon begins to wane, now is the time to show gratitude for what this lunar cycle has brought you so far. Reflect on what worked and what projects are still in progress. Big ambitions take more than one lunar cycle to manifest, so use this time to assess where you are on the path to achievement and reflect on what your next steps should be. Think about what has worked well for you and what you would like to change or do better at in the next lunar cycle.

Last/Third Quarter Moon

This is the time to start releasing anything that no longer serves you. Let go of old grudges, bad relationships, mistakes made, toxic habits and so on. In this phase, the moon requires you to be honest with yourself, to identify the toxic behaviours and bad habits that might be contributing to a negative situation, so that you can release those too.

Waning Crescent/Balsamic Moon

This phase marks the end of the lunar cycle, when the moon shows up in our skies as the classic fairy-tale C-shaped crescent. It is a time to reflect and move deeper into self-awareness. This is a good time to cast banishing spells as the moon's energy helps to pull things away from you (the word "balsamic" in its name refers to its restorative nature). Slowly the light will fade out, night by night, until we are back at the dark moon and the cycle begins once more, so it is never too late for a fresh start and each moon cycle offers a new opportunity to begin again.

CHAPTER THREE

Spellbound

Casting a spell is similar to conducting a science experiment. You gather the apparatus required, use your knowledge and instincts to guide you, and then make a note of what worked well and what didn't, what needs tweaking and so on. Then you repeat the process until you get the results you want, or until you learn something new. Like any other scientific experiment, magic involves certain preparations and it has its own tool kit. No two practitioners will experience exactly the same results, even if they are casting the same spell. This is because magic utilizes your own unique energy and so the way it manifests will be as individual as you are.

Elements of Magic

Most spells combine your own power with that of nature and the universe, using the four elements of earth, air, fire and water. These elements make up the whole of the natural world around us, so adding them into spell-craft is a very powerful approach and one that witches have used for centuries. If you look carefully at any spell book, including this one, you will see these four elements pop up time and again. This is because our survival depends on them, and each is essential to us in its own way. Each element also represents a particular kind of magic. In general, a spell will incorporate at least one of these elements in some form or another. The main tools of magic also link back to one or other of the elements.

Earth

The Earth is our mother and the planet on which we reside so we should take steps to care for and protect her. Earth power is green and growing, ever-changing and renewing. It is the strength of the trees and forest, the growth of plants, the blooming and blossoming of flowers, the darkness of caves and coves, the majesty of mountains. It is alive with potential. In magic, earth power is represented with herbs, plants, leaves, cones, crystals and so on. Earth spells tend to focus on growth, abundance, expansion, transformation and grounding.

Air

Air is vital for our survival. Like the wind, the powers of air can be soft and gentle as a summer breeze, or strong and raging as a winter gale. It can be a tricky power to work with, being so changeable. It is seen in the clouds drifting by, or the flight of birds. It can be felt in the soft brush of falling leaves, blossom and feathers. In magic, the power of air is represented with burning incense, smudge bundles, feathers, fans and images of birds or clouds. Air spells tend to be cast for inspiration, creativity, communication, ambition, momentum and the arts. Music is particularly associated with the powers of air, especially wind instruments.

Fire

The fire of the sun keeps our planet habitable and abundant with fruitful growth. Fire power can be felt on a hot summer day, or in the first rays of sunshine after a long winter. A careful balance must be struck when using fire in spells, because it has the power to destroy and consume everything in its path. In general, fire magic is contained within a heat-proof vessel, such as an iron cauldron, to keep it from getting out of hand. We have all felt the pull of this element — we feel its power when we gaze into the flame of a candle, or when warming ourselves by the fire. In magic, it is naturally represented by burning candles and tea-lights, but it can also be channelled through fiery-coloured crystals, combining the powers of earth and fire in one. Fire spells are cast for passion, love and desire, but due to this element's all-consuming nature, fire magic is used in banishing spells too. If you want to be free of something, then a fire spell will usually do the trick.

Water

Water is the most healing of all the elements. You need only spend a day at the coast to feel its power improving your well-being. Water accounts for 71 per cent of the Earth's surface and up to 60 per cent of the human body, so it is an element that is close to all of us. Again, like air, water can be temperamental — a gentle stream or a destructive tidal wave. Rivers, streams, brooks, burns, lochs, lakes and oceans are all great places to cast water spells. Rain, ice and snow water can also be used, as can your bath and shower at home. In magic, water is represented with a chalice of water or wine, seashells, pebbles, images of fish and marine life. Driftwood and seaweed can also be used, thus combining the elements of water and earth. Water spells are usually cast for matters of emotional balance, healing, dreams, intuition, psychic ability, cleansing and purifying.

Tools of magic

A lthough spells can be successfully performed with relatively few tools, there are several items that most witches keep handy. You will need to gather a set of these tools, but most can be found around the house and adapted to magical use, so there is no need to spend a lot of money.

Athame

This is a magical knife. It is used to direct energy, or to carve sigils and words into spell candles. Traditionally it should have a black handle and the blade should be dulled to render it harmless. You can use any knife that you find appealing, however, from a basic kitchen knife to a fancy letter opener. The athame is attuned with the element of fire.

Wand

A wand can be used as an alternative to the athame, for directing energy. It can be made of crystal or wood and associated with the element of air.

Pentacle

This is a round disc depicting a pentagram or five-pointed star upon it. It is probably the most useful tool of spell-craft, as witches place candles and crystals on the pentacle to charge them with magical energy. It is attuned with the element of earth. You can make one yourself by drawing a five-pointed star on a plate.

Chalice

Your chalice can be any stemmed drinking vessel of your choice. There are lots of magical chalices available, from pretty silver ones to ornate pewter goblets, but a simple wine glass will also suffice. The chalice is attuned with the element of water and used to hold ritual wine.

Broom/Besom

Yes, witches do use broomsticks! A traditional broom is used in cleansing rituals to sweep away negative energy. They are usually decorated with ribbons, feathers and carvings down the stave, and simple ones can be bought quite inexpensively around Halloween, or from garden centres, which you can decorate in your preferred style.

Cauldron

An iron cauldron is typically used to contain fire. This means that you can safely burn fire spells inside, or place a candle in it as part of a ritual celebration. It can also be used as a divination tool. Like the chalice, it represents the element of water. You can pick up iron cauldrons in antique shops, but, for the time being, any fire-proof pan will do.

Cloaks and Crown

These are by no means essential and are reminiscent of high ceremonial magic, such as Wicca, but some magical practitioners do like to wear a special robe, gown or cloak when they are in a ritual setting. Crowns were used to denote hierarchy in a coven, but a simple flower or moon crown can be worn and can help the practitioner to step into a magical frame of mind. Cloaks can be useful when conducting spells and rituals outdoors, especially on cold evenings. It must be stressed, however, that this is down to personal preference and is not a necessary tool of magic.

Consumables

Most of the spells in this book utilize some kind of consumable ingredients, such as herbs, candles, oils, crystals, ribbons and so on. If you are on a budget, this is where you should focus your magical spending, as all the other tools can be found around the home and adapted to magical use. You will find a list of consumables and their magical correspondences later in this chapter, so you will be able to switch one ingredient for another if you need to.

CREATING A MAGICAL ALTAR

Once you have gathered your tools, you are ready to create an altar in your home and dedicate it to your magical practice. This can be a shelf, windowsill or work surface. If you are keeping your craft private, your altar can be hidden away in a cupboard or bureau. If you are open about your interests in spell-craft, you can choose to have your altar on display.

Traditionally, the altar should be placed in the north or east of a room. While every witch's altar is unique, it always represents the four elements, plus divinity, and there are certain standard items that should be placed on it.

You should stand two white candles at either side, towards the back of the altar. These represent the element of fire. Between the two candles, place something that represents divinity to you. This could be a statue of a goddess or a god, or both. It could be a picture of a deity in a nice frame, or it could be something more abstract, such as a beautiful crystal or a plant.

An incense holder of some kind is very useful, as you can use it to represent the element of air, and also to burn incense sticks as an offering of thanks, even when you don't plan on casting a full ritual. Place the incense holder to the east or right side of the altar.

Water is usually represented by a chalice. This can be any stemmed drinking vessel, placed at the west or left side of the altar. As an alternative, you can use a beautiful seashell or pebble. Finally, you should add something to represent the element of earth. This could be a plant, crystal, flowers or your pentacle, which belongs front and centre of the altar.

Other items that you might like to use as decoration for your altar include crystals, seashells, feathers, pine cones or a jar of salt for purification. Make it as magical and beautiful as you can, and place your Book of Spells close by. Be aware that your altar will evolve over time as you grow into your magic.

Symbols of Magic

Certain symbols and sigils are seen time and again in magic, each one with its own special meaning. Below is a list of the most common symbols used in magical practice, though this is by no means exhaustive. There might also be symbols that you feel drawn to that do not feature on this list, but you should feel free to experiment with those too.

Pentagram

This is the magical five-pointed star, not to be confused with the Star of David, which has six points. The pentagram is the most common symbol used in magic. It is carved upon the pentacle disc, into candles, written on spell papers and so on. It represents the forces of positive magic, with each point of the star being associated with one of the elements and the top point representing the energy of the universe or the light of spirit and divinity.

Reverse Pentagram

Thanks to horror films, the reverse pentagram has something of a bad reputation, being much maligned in popular culture; non-magical people tend to associate it with negative types of magic. In Wiccan circles however, the reverse pentagram — two points upwards and one point facing downwards — has nothing to do with negative magic or evil influences.

If you look closely at the reverse pentagram, you will see that the shape suggests the horns and beard of the Horned God of Wicca, so it used to attune with the male aspect of nature and divinity. There is nothing at all sinister about this symbol and it can be used in positive magic or in meditation to reflect on the reverse energies of nature, such as darkness, decay and winter. That said, the pop-culture associations are well known in society, so be mindful of these negative associations and use the reverse pentagram carefully, as it can make people a little nervous.

The Triple Goddess

The sigil of the Triple Goddess is used in magic to connect spells with the divine feminine and with the triple aspects of womanhood: Maiden, Mother and Crone. It is another popular symbol that frequently comes up in spells and rituals.

The Triquetra

This is another symbol of trinity and the divine female, yet it can also be used to represent the past, present and future, symbolizing the interwoven thread that links all three together.

Ankh

This Egyptian symbol is often seen in magical circles and has become a popular sigil, used to represent immortality, reincarnation, afterlife and the sacred journey of the undying, eternal spirit.

Eye of Horus

Another Egyptian symbol, this time associated with wisdom, clarity, the spiritual vision of the third eye, psychic ability and the realms of the unseen. It is often used as a protection device, to guard against all harm, both seen and unseen.

Equal-Armed Cross

This sigil symbolizes the meeting of the four directions, the four winds and the four elements. It is also used to represent the four seasonal thresholds of Spring Equinox, Midsummer, Autumnal Equinox and Midwinter. It is used in magic for grounding and stability. It is associated with polarity and duality.

Celtic Cross

The Celtic Cross embodies all the symbolism of the Equal-Armed Cross, yet it also has the protective powers of the sacred circle, making this a very powerful symbol indeed.

Magical Correspondences

A ny tool that is used in spell-craft is called a correspondence. There are correspondences for all different types of magic and you will need to know what these are when you come to start writing your own spells. Below is a list of magical correspondences for the most popular types of magic, so that if you don't have what a spell calls for, you can switch to something else that has the same associations. This should work just as well and it will stand you in good stead when you come to write your own spells. Of course, if you have had great success with a particular herb or crystal, then keep using it.

MAGICAL CORRESPONDENCES FOR LOVE

Colours	Red, pink, lilac, white
Crystals	Carnelian, rose quartz, ruby, diamond, clear quartz, citrine
Herbs	Rose, rosemary, peony, lavender, lilac, elder flower, myrtle, ivy
Oils	Rose, geranium, ylang-ylang, lavender, neroli
Incense	Rose, strawberry, ylang-ylang, night queen, sandalwood

MAGICAL CORRESPONDENCES FOR PROSPERITY

Colours	Green, gold, silver, white
Crystals	Aventurine, jade, iron pyrite, clear quartz
Herbs	Basil, bay, cinnamon, tea leaves, sage, mint, sunflower
Oils	Patchouli, frankincense, sunflower, rape seed
Incense	Cinnamon, frankincense, night queen, patchouli, dragon's blood

MAGICAL CORRESPONDENCES FOR PROTECTION

Colours	Black, grey, dark blue, purple, dark red, white
Crystals	Haematite, onyx, amethyst, sodalite, smoky quartz
Herbs	Thistle, rosemary, basil, holly, turmeric, garlic, mugwort, foxglove
Oils	Tea tree, bergamot, eucalyptus, cedar wood, pine
Incense	Pine, sage, night queen, patchouli, dragon's blood, black pepper

MAGICAL CORRESPONDENCES FOR POWER

Colours	Black, purple, red, white
Crystals	Haematite, amethyst, clear quartz, smoky quartz, snowy quartz
Herbs	Lavender, rosemary, basil, sage, mugwort
Oils	Tea tree, patchouli, eucalyptus, pine
Incense	Pine, sage, night queen, patchouli, dragon's blood

Creating a Sacred Space

Most practitioners of magic cast their spells in a special space that has been ritually constructed and cleansed. This need not be an elaborate or large space; a small area of a room or a quiet, sheltered spot out of doors are both more than adequate. This space should give you access to the altar, or enable you to set up one on the ground if you prefer to work outside. To begin with, smudge the area with incense, by wafting an incense stick or a smudge bundle around the entire sacred space. This acts as a ritual cleansing.

All magic is performed within the protective space of this type of cast circle, which is a visualization exercise. The circle of magic is a realm between the worlds, which means that it hangs in the ether, deep within the womb of sacred creativity, creating a portal which allows the magic of transformation to be birthed. The circle is where all magic begins and the seeds of manifestation are sown. It is often referred to as being between the worlds, meaning that it is of both the magical and mundane realms of existence.

The purpose of the circle is to contain the energy that you raise as you work magic, so that it doesn't leak away from the spell. In this way the magical energy is only released when the practitioner directs and wills it to be so. The circle also acts as a boundary of protection around you as you work. A magic circle can be cast as a protective device around your home, your car or yourself too, so it is a handy skill to acquire.

CASTING A CIRCLE

To cast a circle, you will need your athame, wand or finger. Stand before your altar and walk, or turn if the spacc is small, in a circle with your wand (or whatever) held out. Move three times in a clockwise direction, visualizing a blue or white light coming from your athame, wand or finger and creating a circle all around you and your altar. As you do so, say:

I conjure this circle of sacred power
Protect my magic this witching hour
In the great void of darkness, I conjure this shield
In my magical fortress, this circle is sealed.

CALLING THE QUARTERS

Each quarter of the circle is governed by one of the elements. These elements should also be called, or invoked, before any magic is performed. As spell-craft is all about attuning with nature, we invoke the four elements that make up our world — earth, air, fire and water. To begin the invocations, go to the north of your circle, raise your arms high in invocation and say:

> Elemental guardians of the north
> Powers of abundance and growth
> I invoke your presence and ask you
> to protect this sacred space.

Move to the east of the circle and repeat the process, saying,

> Elemental guardians of the east
> Powers of creativity and communication
> I invoke your presence and ask you
> to protect this sacred space.

Move to the south of your circle and this time say,

> Elemental guardians of the south
> Powers of love and passion
> I invoke your presence and ask you
> to protect this sacred space.

Finally, go to the west of the circle and invoke the final quarter saying,

> Elemental guardians of the west
> Powers of intuition and emotion
> I invoke your presence and ask you
> to protect this sacred space.

Move to the middle of the circle and say,

> Welcome, spirits and guardians four
> To this world between worlds of magical lore.

You are now ready to work rituals with your chosen deities, cast the spells of your choice spells or perform divinations. Once you have completed your magical tasks, you will need to release all the guardians that you have invoked. Do this by going in reverse order, starting in the west, and saying to each quarter,

> The spell is cast, the magic is bright
> Guardians I release you
> In peace, love and light.

TO TAKE DOWN THE CIRCLE

Once the magic is complete and the element guardians have been released, you need to take down the magic circle that you have created. This is an indication that your spell has been released into the world so that it can begin to manifest. Taking down the circle is easy. Simply walk three times around your sacred space in an anti-clockwise direction, imagining the light of the circle fading out as you say:

The wise words of spell-craft have now been spoken

This circle is open, but never broken.

You can now go about your normal daily routine, knowing that you have added a touch of magic and enchantment to your life.

CHAPTER FOUR

Casting for Mental Health and Resilience

One of the most important things you can ever do as a magical practitioner is work on your mental health and robustness. This is because you need a calm and balanced mind in order to cast effective spells. A wise witch is a strong witch and strong witches do not crumble at the first hurdle or disappointment. They know who they are and what they want from life. They have an awareness of their own faults and they work steadily to try and improve them. They know what they expect from themselves and from others. This is not to say that they are perfect and never have a bad day. Of course they do, but they understand that they have a role to play in resolving any issues that come up.

Good mental health is about ensuring that you have more good days than bad ones, and that you build up a resilience so that you can cope with the darker days more effectively. It is about restoring a level of balance, both in your moods and in your daily habits. You need to feel productive for your own self-esteem, but you also need time to rest on the bad days when your mental health takes a knock.

Restoring this balance in your mental health can be enhanced with spell-craft and positive exercises. This isn't about denying the issues you might be facing — it is about acknowledging that you have a particular challenge, be it anxiety, depression or low self-esteem, and offering coping strategies to help you deal with it. While a detailed exploration of mental health and self-care is beyond the scope of this chapter, you can learn more about facing these issues from my book *A Wiccan Guide to Self-Care*. Here, however, we will explore magical ways for you to increase your overall resilience and robustness, and to restore the balance of your mind-set for greater mental well-being.

DARK CRYSTAL SPELL TO ABSORB A NEGATIVE THOUGHT SPIRAL

Items required: A black obsidian or smoky quartz crystal

Timing: Perform when you identify a negative thought spiral

First of all, remove yourself from the situation and find a quiet space. Keep a black crystal with you if you know that you are prone to negative thought spirals. Once in your quiet place, take the crystal and hold it close to your lips. Breathe out all the negative emotions, and visualize the dark crystal absorbing those energies. These darker crystals are very good for absorbing negativity and neutralizing it, so keep breathing your panic into the crystal until a state of calmness is restored. Immediately afterwards, rinse the crystal in cold running water to cleanse away all the negativity. As an alternative, if you don't have a black crystal handy, you can breathe the negative panic into a tissue and then flush it away.

SPELL TO TURN A NEGATIVE INTO A POSITIVE

Items required: A black or white board, chalk or a dry-wipe marker pen, a cloth

Timing: Best performed during the dark moon

On the board write a word that sums up your negative self-talk, such as worthlessness, friendless or stupid. Write it in big letters. Sometimes you need to see something written down to fully understand its impact on you. Sit for a moment and look at that word. This is what you are telling yourself every day.

Imagine if someone was saying that to someone you love — what would you do? How would you defend that person? What would you say to make them feel better? Come up with a single word that is the opposite of the one on the board. Using the examples given above, you might choose worthy, popular or intelligent.

As the final step, rub out the negative word and replace it with the positive one, then set the board where you can see it every day. Each time you catch yourself using negative words to, and about, yourself, replace them with positive ones. You can repeat this spell as a visualization exercise whenever you need to — just imagine the board in your mind and rub out the negative words to replace them with more positive ones.

Dealing with Anxiety

Anxiety is the result of a negative thought spiral. It is the emotional response to the mind's catastrophizing. Sometimes anxiety is natural and valid — if you are having a job interview, for instance. The problem occurs when anxiety becomes prolonged or habitual, and shows up uninvited for no good reason.

Stress is a part of daily life, but it's one that we must take steps to minimize and counteract. If you have severe anxiety, of course, go and see your doctor, but, for everyday stress, remedies such as bath potions can work wonders. Because, when you are feeling particularly stressed or anxious, you won't have the energy for a full ritual, bath potions can be made up in advance and kept in an airtight jar, ready for use when you need them most.

A RESTORATIVE LAVENDER BATH POTION

Items required: A voile pouch, muslin cloth or hankie, two teaspoons of dried lavender, one teaspoon of dried camomile flowers, a lavender ribbon, lavender essential oil

Timing: Use this spell whenever you are feeling particularly stressed, but it works all the better at a full moon

For this restorative bath potion, you will need two parts dried lavender, mixed with one part dried camomile flowers. Both these herbs are well known for their healing and restful properties. If there is a more restful way to de-stress than soaking in a fragrant lavender bath, I haven't found it yet!

First make the bathroom enticing. Light candles and run a hot bath. Place the dried herbs into the pouch, or in the middle of the hankie and tie it tightly using the ribbon. As the bath fills, swirl the pouch of herbs in the water in a clockwise direction, scenting the hot water. Tie the pouch to the tap so that it hangs in the water.

As a final step, add ten drops of lavender essential oil to the water just before you sink into the depths. Relax and breath in the fragrance. Allow the herbal scent to calm you and let go of any stressful thoughts. Remain in the water for as long as you can, making the most of the restful energies of the herbs. When you are ready, dry off and empty the wet herbs into the earth, giving back what you have taken. Enjoy the remainder of your day and do calming, gentle activities to maintain your sense of peace. You can also use this pouch in a shower, hanging it by the shower head and letting the steam release the scents.

Dealing with Depression

Depression is a deep sense of sorrow, usually accompanied by low self-worth. In extreme cases it can be triggered by a chemical imbalance in the brain, which you will need to consult a doctor about to seek treatment. However, most people will experience milder forms of depression at some point during their lifetime.

In almost all cases of depression, it is worth going to see your doctor, but there are also things that you can do yourself to help alleviate the symptoms, such as taking a walk or other forms of regular exercise, enjoying a restorative bath or shower using the lavender potion above or talking to someone, be it a friend, relative, doctor, therapist or all of the above.

A FIRE SPELL TO ALLEVIATE DEPRESSION

Items required: A notepad, a pen, a lighter, a cauldron or heat-proof bowl

Timing: During the waning moon

For this spell you will need some time in solitude. Have your phone handy, so you can call someone if you need to, but mute it so you are not disturbed. Take a moment and think about the depression you might be experiencing and try to identify the main event that triggered it. Write down an account of that event, how it makes you feel, what emotions come up for you when you remember it. Note down how the feelings of low mood are impacting on your life and self-image. Write it all out, whatever comes up. Get it all out on paper, where you can see it. This is all the stuff that you have been carrying around in your head and your heart. Release it onto the page. When you are done, read it through. Now roll up the paper, light it and allow it to burn in the cauldron. As you do so, say:

> My past no longer binds me tight
> From my woes I'm free
> I let it go to set things right
> As I will it so shall it be.

Once the paper has burnt and cooled, throw the ashes out into the wind and let it all go.

The Trick to Happiness

Happiness is brought about through four things — something to do, someone to love, something to look forward to and gratitude for all of the above. It sounds like a very simple recipe, so shouldn't we all be happy every day? Too often, people tend to focus on the negatives instead, latching on to their disappointments when they should be making plans for new achievements and events.

Having something to do isn't only about a career or job, it can be a hobby or volunteering. Someone to love could be a pet, an elderly neighbour, a tank of fish or even a potted plant. Something to look forward to is probably the easiest one to master as we can all plan a night out, a theatre trip or a holiday. Gratitude should be a daily habit, because once you begin to notice these smaller moments of joy, that is when your happiness will grow and you will feel truly blessed. So take a moment right now and see if you can tick off all four criteria for happiness in *your* life.

Building Resilience

If good mental health is all about robustness, how do you go about building up your resilience? Life is a fantastic teacher and the lessons you most need to learn will just come to you. In Wiccan circles we believe that people are never given more than they can handle, but you might be stretched almost to breaking point. Crime, poverty, food insecurity, job losses, bereavements and illness are all lessons and opportunities for you to increase your resilience. Difficult times are when you are being smelted in the fire and made stronger. Try to lean into them and see how resilient you can become. In the meantime, cast this spell for greater strength and courage.

A SPELL FOR INNER STRENGTH

Items required: A thistle, a cord or ribbon on which to hang it, a thistle pendant

Timing: On the waxing moon

The thistle is the flower of Scotland and its motto is "None shall irritate me unscathed," meaning that it will inflict the swift retribution of its prickles to anyone who dares tamper with it! This is a good metaphor for developing inner strength. No one can cause you lasting harm if you face them with courage and move forward in your life with resilience. On the night of the waxing moon, take a thistle flower and hold it to your heart. Bow your head in reverence and say:

I choose to live by the law of the thistle
I make this promise by night
To face each foe without fear
To let my courage take flight
From hardship and want I'll not waver
From conflict I will not flinch
As I wear my thistle favour
My strength grows inch by inch
So mote it be.

To complete the spell, tie the ribbon around the thistle and hang it upside down to dry, somewhere close to your altar, or your bed, if possible. Put on the thistle necklace and wear it as a talisman of inner strength.

A SILENT SPELL FOR RESILIENCE

Items required: A small square of paper, a few pine needles or a small clipping from a fir tree or evergreen plant, sealing wax

Timing: Best performed on the new moon

Gather the items together and sit for a while contemplating how it feels to be resilient. When troubles come, you can cope with them; when conflict appears, you can emerge victorious; when facing a challenge, you know that you are capable. Picture all of this in your mind and envision yourself as a strong, resilient, capable individual. Now place the pine needles or the evergreen in the centre of the paper. Evergreens can weather most storms — they bend in the wind rather than breaking, they show their true colours in the darkest time of winter — so they are a good representation of the kind of reliance you are casting for. Once the evergreens are in place, fold each of the corners of the paper inwards, covering the greenery and forming a small parcel. Seal the corners together by dripping sealing wax where they meet. This is your charm for resilience. Let it sit in the light of the moon for a full lunar cycle, then keep it close to you whenever you are going through a challenging time.

CHAPTER FIVE

Casting for Dreams, Goals and Ambitions

Having dreams, goals and ambitions is an important aspect of keeping your life moving forwards. Without a goal to aim for, life can become monotonous, routine and stagnant. Goal-setting is an intrinsic part of spell-craft, but it should also be considered an intrinsic part of life. You need to know where you are heading and what you want before you can start casting for it. Without a clear direction, you will be buffeted by the whims of others, and you might find yourself growing resentful when those around you achieve their dreams but you don't seem to be getting anywhere. This chapter will help you to determine what it is that you want from life and offers magical steps towards achieving it.

SPELL TO LIGHT THE SPARK OF AMBITION

Items required: A gold or silver candle and suitable holder, your athame or carving tool, sunflower oil, a little saffron (optional)

Timing: Cast at noon, during the time of the full moon for greatest power of sun and moon energy

Take the items to your altar and think about what it means to be ambitious. How would you feel if you believed that you could achieve anything? What would your life look like? Imagine how much confidence you would have. Try to dream up these feelings as you hold the candle in your hands.

Visualize yourself living out your dreams and achieving your goals. When you are ready, carve the word "Ambition" into the length of the candle, then anoint it by rubbing the sunflower oil all over it, imbuing the candle with the sun's energies. If you are using saffron, sprinkle a little onto some kitchen towel and roll the anointed candle through the saffron so that it sticks to the oil, pulling the candle towards you as you do so. You only need a small amount of saffron because it is very powerful. Place the candle into the holder and light the wick as you chant these words nine times:

> Ambition burns bright in me
> The light of success shines down upon me
> The sunlight empowers me
> The moonlight guides me
> Opportunity finds me
> Achievement delights me
> By earth, moon and sun
> This magic is done.

Leave the candle in place to burn down naturally, which can take several hours, so make sure you cast this spell when you will be at home to watch over the flame.

What Do You Really, Really Want?

Half the fun of having ambition lies in deciding exactly what you want. This is where you get to dream up a variety of possibilities and see which one calls to you the loudest. If you could make your living in a fun way, what would you be doing? If you could live anywhere, with any lifestyle, what would that be? If you could meet one of your idols, who would you choose?

Spending time visualizing is all part of the creative, magical process. You have to be able to envision something before you can bring it into being. Remember that manifesting anything is a collaboration and you must play your part. Decide what you want most and start to work towards that goal. A smaller goal is usually achieved more easily, so start with something simple to increase your confidence and then work up to the bigger goals. Once you have a clear idea of your main goals, use that information to create a vision board.

CREATE A MAGICAL VISION BOARD

Items required: A large piece of poster board, images that represent your ambitions, a glue stick, patchouli oil, a marker pen

Timing: Create your board at the time of the new moon, to bring all good things towards you

Making a vision board is a traditional way to set your intention and have your goals in front of you on a daily basis. While you can make digital versions on a computer, you will need to anoint your board with oil, so the old-fashioned poster-board variety is necessary for this spell. Find images that represent the things you are working towards –such as pictures of people working from home, travelling or enjoying a romantic dinner. Gather a collection of images, so that all the main aspects of your life are represented. Alternatively, you can create a vision board that focuses on a single ambition or goal.

Using the marker pen, draw a pentagram on the back of the board. This will help to protect your dreams from negative energies and toxic influences. Take the patchouli oil, which represents success and abundance, and dab a little onto the four corners of the vision board. Next, glue all the images in place on the board and put it where you will see it every day.

This board should act as a reminder to you, inspiring you to keep your dreams in mind and work towards them every day. As you achieve the goals on the board, use a red, silver or gold pen to tick them off. This will give you a boost, as you see that you are moving closer to your dreams, one step at a time. Once the board is full of ticks and you have checked off all the images, make a new board designed around your new goals.

SEVEN-STEP SPELL FOR GOAL MANIFESTATION

Items required: Seven slips of paper, a special tea-light holder, tea-lights, a pen

Timing: At the time of the full moon

This is an ongoing spell that takes time to complete so you will need to include it in your day-to-day routine. It works best for bigger goals, such as changing careers, moving house, starting a family and so on.

Gather the items needed and begin by visualizing the goal as if you were already living it. Enjoy this part of the process and indulge in a little daydreaming. What does your goal feel like to you? How does it make you act, dress, behave? Once you can see the goal clearly, break it down into seven manageable steps to get you there and write step on each of the slips of paper.

You now have seven pieces of paper which spell out what you need to do to achieve your goal. Take the first piece of paper and read the first step out loud. This is an instruction to yourself, a command to make the first move and to get the ball rolling.

Light a tea-light in the holder each evening and place all the spell papers close by. Each day, follow the command of the relevant step until you

74

have achieved that aspect of the goal, then burn it in the flame of the tea-light. In burning the spell paper, you are indicating that you cannot go backwards, but can only move forwards towards your goal.

Lucky, Lucky, Lucky

There is more to a successful ambition than just hard work and goal-setting. At some stage, luck and good fortune will also play a part, putting you in the right place at the right time. There is also much to be said for knowing the right people and moving in the right circles, although not everyone has such connections. So how can you get ahead when you are still on the outside looking in, when your goal still seems like more of a pipe-dream? Here are a few mundane tips that you can use to start turning luck in your favour:

* **Be nice to the gatekeepers.** In all your dealings with your chosen industry or ambition, be nice to receptionists, personal assistants, secretaries and so on. They are the gatekeepers to the world you wish to join and they are the ones who can ensure your correspondence reaches the right people, so be nice. They can open doors you didn't even know existed!

* **Use a charm offensive.** Aim to be pleasant and personable in all your interactions, and your name is more likely to be remembered for all the right reasons when new opportunities are up for grabs.

* **Don't just offer your services.** You need to offer something concrete, rather than just the gift of your services, as

this can come across as being condescending. Offer a business plan, a submission, a proposal, a demonstration — something that proves you have put some thought into how you can be an asset.

Think of all this as laying the groundwork. In any given day, you never know who you might meet and it only takes one person to like you for doors to start swinging wide open in welcome. That said, Lady Luck tends to bestow her gifts where she is most at home, so you need to believe that fortune favours you.

A SPELL FOR GOOD FORTUNE

Items required: An ace of diamonds playing card, frankincense oil, a pen

Timing: During a waxing moon

Playing cards have long been used in spell-casting, so it is always a good idea to have an extra pack around the house. This spell calls for the ace of diamonds. Pick it up and write your full name and date of birth on the front of the card. Dab it with a touch of frankincense oil on all four corners. Put the playing card face up on your pentacle and place your hands palms up to receive, on either side of the pentacle.

Sit for a time and imagine lots of luck coming to you. Visualize meeting the right people, receiving invitations, having the right opportunities extended to you. Imagine winning streaks, lucky breaks, windfalls and blessings, all coming to you now. When you feel ready chant the following words three times:

Lady Luck shines bright on me
All my dreams come true
In love and light there comes to me
Diamonds forged anew
Fate will open doors for me
This charm now paves the way
Opportunities now come to me
My luck is strong by night and day.

HOW TO MAKE FORTUNA OIL

Items required: A 50ml (1¾fl oz) bottle and stopper, 40ml (1¼fl oz) sweet almond oil, frankincense, patchouli and citronella essential oils, three small threads of saffron, a small lodestone crystal (tiny enough to fit in the bottle), a Night Queen incense stick

Timing: Prepare this oil at the time of the full moon

In Greek mythology, Fortuna was the goddess of luck and fortune. She was said to wear a blindfold, which made her impartial to whoever received the luck she doled out. This magical oil can be used to anoint spell candles, cards, crystals and charms. You can also use a small amount of it as a bath oil.

On the night of the full moon, first cleanse the bottle by lighting the stick of incense and putting the smouldering tip into the jar. Let the vessel fill with cleansing smoke, then set the incense stick to one side to burn safely as you work. Next drop the lodestone, which is a natural magnet, into the bottle to attract great opportunities to you. Add the saffron threads to bring good fortune your way. Pour in the sweet almond oil, then add five drops each of the following essential oils: frankincense, patchouli and citronella. Put the stopper in the bottle to seal it. Then hold it on your hands and empower it to its purpose with the following incantation.

Lady Fortuna, goddess of old
Through lodestone and saffron more precious than gold
Through citron, patchouli and incense of kings
Your gift of good fortune this oil now brings
Lady Fortuna, smile on me this night
That I may bring my ambitions forth into the light
So mote it be.

SILENT SPELL
TO BOTTLE YOUR DREAMS

Items required: A small spell jar 2.5–5cm (1–2 inches) tall with a stopper, a tiny slip of paper, a pen, silver thread, a silver candle or sealing wax, dried basil, cinnamon and sage, a clipping of your hair, a Night Queen incense stick to cleanse

Timing: On the new moon

To begin with, cleanse the jar using the stick of incense following the instructions above. Think of a single key word that sums up your main goal or dream. Write this on the slip of paper, then roll the paper into a small scroll and secure it with the silver thread. Drop it into the jar, add the hair clipping, then use equal amounts of the three dried herbs to fill the jar. Fix the spell in place with the stopper and seal it by dripping hot wax around the neck and stopper of the jar.

Keep the jar in a special place. Once your dream has manifested, break the seal and tip the contents of the jar into the earth and bury them, giving thanks for your good fortune. Wash the jar, cleaning off all the old wax, so that you can use it again for future containment spells. Remember to cleanse it with incense before you use it again.

The spells in this chapter can used alone or in conjunction with other spells in this book. By layering up spell-craft in this way, you have a greater chance of success. When building a ritual, choose one of these generic spells for ambition and goal-setting, along with a spell from the relevant chapter, say a love spell, to bring about the manifestation of your desire. Happy casting!

CHAPTER SIX

Casting for Abundance

Money is an issue for many people. Too much of it can be overwhelming, while too little can lead to destitution. There are very few people who are entirely comfortable with the amount of money they have; most people have some degree of money stress to contend with. While money should never be thought of as the root of all evil, it can be troublesome at times. In this chapter we will explore how you can use magic to become more abundant and prosperous, so that your money worries are few and fleeting.

Casting for Money and Prosperity

It is an acceptable practice to cast spells for money, but there are a few things to bear in mind. First of all, you should cast money spells based on need, not greed, because the sense of urgency to get your needs met will make the spell more powerful. Casting to win a lottery jackpot with the vague notion that you would like to be rich is unlikely to succeed, because there is no genuine emotional need driving the spell.

Money spells can manifest in a myriad of ways — more overtime at work, a pay rise, a tax rebate, a windfall. It won't usually be "free money" that comes to you out of the blue, but it will be money that you have either worked for or overpaid. That said, sometimes a windfall will come to you after a prosperity spell has been cast and this always feels very magical, but it is more usual that you will need to participate in acquiring additional cash, even with magic on your side.

As money can sometimes come through negative routes such as insurance pay-outs and compensation, it is always wise to add a simple caveat to all your money spells to ensure that any money coming your way comes through positive means and with harm to none. So at the end of every spell for abundance you should say:

I cast this spell with harm to none
For the good of all, so it be done.

This will ensure that all your prosperity spells work in a nice, gentle manner and via a positive means of manifestation.

How Much Do You Need?

It is surprising how many people don't actually know how much money they need to live on each month, or how much they spend on non-essentials. This is vital information and it is the first thing you need to determine, before you begin casting money spells. There is no point in casting for more money if you have no clue where your current income is going. Are you really not making enough to live on, or are you simply over-spending?

So the first step is to work out exactly how much money you need to pay all your bills, keep the car running and buy groceries for the month. Add all these expenses together to come up with a single figure. This is your baseline, your survival money. If your income is below this threshold, you are not making enough money. If it is above, but only just, you are still in a precarious position. If you have quite a bit more than your baseline but you struggle financially nonetheless, you are probably over-spending and you need to work out where your frivolous spending zones are.

Once you have your baseline figure, you can work out how much you want to start saving for your margin of happiness, or towards a specific event such as a wedding, Christmas funds or a holiday. This in turn will determine how much extra money you need to bring in each month, which is the figure you should base your spell-casting around. Alternatively, you can cast for a sum of money to cover the cost of a large purchase such as a new appliance.

SPELL TO MAKE A GENERAL PROSPERITY POUCH

Items required: A green pouch, three silver coins, a lodestone crystal, half a cinnamon stick

Timing: On the new moon

This spell works to keep prosperity flowing towards you at all times. Place the items on your pentacle to charge overnight as the new moon first appears. The next day, hold the coins and the crystal in your hands and say:

> Coins of silver shining bright
> Bring forth to me by new moon light
> The gift of great prosperity
> This lodestone draws it here to me
> In peace and plenty I will thrive
> My increased wealth now comes alive!

Place the coins and crystal in the pouch, then using the cinnamon stick, trace a pound or dollar sign on the pouch and put the cinnamon stick inside to draw money to you. Keep this prosperity pouch near you as you sleep, to keep money flowing to you.

A SILENT TEA OF PLENTY SPELL TO EASE MONEY WORRIES

Items required: A cup of peppermint tea

Timing: Use this spell whenever you feel anxious about money

Peppermint is the herb of plenty, strongly associated with abundance and prosperity. Make a cup of peppermint tea in your favourite mug. Find a quiet place and sit with the tea. Breath in the scent of mint and try to calm your money worries. Think back to other times when you were just as worried about making ends meet, but remember how you made it through. Know that you will find a way to get through any lean times you might experience and trust that something will always turn up to help you. Imagine paying all your bills easily and having plenty of food to eat. Feel an emotion of plenty filling you as you sip the peppermint tea and take its gifts of prosperity into yourself. You and the mint are one; it fills you with abundance and hope. It warms you through with its comforting heat; it refreshes you for the time ahead. When you are finished with the tea, scatter the mint leaves in a garden or potted plant and give it back to the earth, with thanks.

SPELL FOR A SPECIFIC SUM OF MONEY

Items required: A green candle and holder, athame or carving tool, patchouli oil, dried mint, paper kitchen towel

Timing: During new to full moon

If there is something you need a specific sum of money for, say a holiday or a special purchase, then cast this spell as the moon waxes from new to full. Visualize what you want the money for and see yourself enjoying that event or item. Take a green candle and carve into the wax the amount of money you require. Anoint the candle in patchouli oil, by rubbing the oil from the top to the middle of the candle, then from the bottom to the middle. This will help to bring the money to you from all directions. Sprinkle a small amount of dried mint on a sheet of paper kitchen towel and roll the candle through the herb, pulling it towards you as you do so. Maintain your visualization throughout this process. Finally, place the candle in the holder, light the wick and say the incantation below, then allow the candle to burn out naturally.

Blessings of wealth come hither from there
I call forth abundance to fly through the air
Circle about and surround me with glee
The sum I require now comes to me!

A PROSPERITY BATH

Items required: A green pouch or hankie, dried mint, a cinnamon stick, a piece of ginger root, a few coins, a green ribbon

Timing: Use this bathing spell on the night of the full moon

Place the coins in the pouch or the middle of the hankie. Add a teaspoon of dried mint, the cinnamon stick and ginger root. These are all associated with prosperity and abundance. Tie the pouch or hankie into a bundle and hang it from the hot tap as you draw a bath, letting the water run over the pouch and release the scents. You can also leave the pouch in the water to infuse if you want to. Enjoy a relaxing bath, soaking in the waters of prosperity. This will cloak you in the energies of abundance and as like attracts like, you will draw more prosperity to you like a magnet. To keep money flowing towards you, perform this bathing ritual every couple of months or so and at least once a quarter.

GROW YOUR OWN ABUNDANCE

Items required: A small mint plant, a plant pot, three aventurine crystals

Timing: On the new moon

Mint is one of the most powerful herbs for attracting prosperity, which is why it features in so many money spells. It is also remarkably easy to grow — either in your garden, if you have one, or on a sunny windowsill. Once you have chosen your plant, pot it up and put the three aventurine crystals on top of the soil around the base of the plant. This will add to the abundance magic that you are creating. Care for the mint, envisioning it bringing wealth and plenty to you, and as it grows your sense of abundance should grow with it. This ritual has the added benefit that you can use the mint for your money spells and in cooking too.

A SPELL FOR MONEY WISDOM

Items required: A piece of iron pyrite also known as fool's gold, a sage smudge bundle and lighter, your wallet or purse, all your bank cards, your pentacle

You work hard for your money and put it to good use, but frivolous spending habits can leave you feeling the pinch if you're not careful. Sometimes it's easy to get carried away and spend too much. However, being wise with your money and considering your purchases carefully before you buy anything will lead to a greater sense of prosperity and control of your finances. Cast this spell to help you to achieve greater wisdom in your financial life.

Gather together all your cards, along with your purse or wallet. Place them on the pentacle, light the smudge bundle and waft the smoke all around the cards and purse to cleanse them of any negative money habits that you might have acquired. Imagine having the discipline to only buy essential purchases and to leave shops or close down web browsers without buying anything. Think of what you could do with the money you save, simply by being more discerning in your shopping habits. Imagine making wise investments with your money or having a healthy savings account. Keep smudging your cards as you envision yourself growing in financial wisdom. When you are ready, pick up the fool's gold and say:

A fool with money I shall not be
No longer spending frivolously
I keep these cards close to my chest
And with prosperity I am blessed.

Keep the fool's gold in your purse or wallet to act as a reminder to be more careful with your money.

Magical Tips to Keep the Money Flowing In

* Put a bay leaf in your purse to ensure it is never empty.

* Carry a lodestone in your pocket to keep your pockets full.

* Carry a conker to draw natural abundance your way.

* Drink mint tea often to take prosperity into yourself.

* Keep aventurine crystals on your desk at work to increase earnings.

* Put the king and queen of diamonds playing cards in your wallet or purse to guard your wealth.

CHAPTER SEVEN

Casting for Career and Business Success

You spend approximately one third of your life at work so it is vital that you enjoy your job as much as possible. Sadly, this isn't the case for many people and, while working for a living is a fact of life, it isn't always easy. That said, there are still practical things you can do to alleviate your situation, if you're not happy. First of all, communicate clearly with your employer: have a meeting and explain that the overtime is too much for you, for example. If your employer is willing to meet you halfway and accommodate your request, all well and good. If they are not, at least now you are aware that your workplace is skewed entirely to one side, which is not in your favour, so brush up your CV and start job-hunting, because they are unlikely to change.

In the meantime, keep your mind above the fray, maintain strong boundaries around your personal time and know your rights. That way you can tread water in a bad job, while at the same time working on your plan of escape. Use the spells and rituals in this chapter to help make your working life more successful and fulfilling. Good luck!

SPELL TO TRANSITION FROM A BAD JOB TO A DREAM JOB

Items required: A notebook and pen, a black candle, athame or carving tool, a white candle, two plates, black pepper and white rice

Timing: On the full moon

It can be very debilitating when you feel trapped in a job that you dislike. However, leaving might not be an option until you have found something else, so use this spell to make that transition a little easier. Write down all that you require from your ideal job, noting down everything you're looking for, from the hours and pay to the environment and kind of colleagues you prefer to work with. Next carve the words "My Dream Job" on the white candle and your current place of employment on the black candle. Set each of these candles on the plates, melting the bottoms of both so that they stand securely. Put the plates side by side. Sprinkle a circle of black pepper around the black candle to banish the negative influence of your current workplace, then sprinkle a circle of white rice for prosperity around the white candle to help manifest your dream job. Light the black candle and say:

> My work is done within this place
> My time here will soon be done
> I walk away with joy and grace
> Happy to be moving on!

Spend a few minutes visualizing your final day at your current workplace, with all your colleagues wishing you well for your future role. When you can see this clearly, light the white candle and say:

> I summon my dream job to me
> In a role that I enjoy
> I call this opportunity
> With the magic I now deploy.

Finally, burn the slip of notepaper describing your dream job in the flame of the white candle. You can begin the transition by actively job-hunting and seeking out new opportunities, but this spell should work within six months.

SILENT SPELL TO SHINE IN AN INTERVIEW

Items required: A pentacle, a small item that you will wear to the interview, a citrine crystal for luck and communication, a pen and paper

Timing: The day before the interview

Job interviews can be very nerve-racking and it can be easy to let them overwhelm you. Preparation is the key to success and the more interviews you do, the more comfortable you will become. Once you have prepared yourself in practical ways, such as researching the company with which you're interviewing and reminding yourself of times you've performed particularly well in your previous or current role, you are ready to cast the spell. Take a small item that you plan to wear to the interview, such as a lipstick, tie or piece of jewellery and place it on the pentacle. Add the citrine crystal, which is good for communication and success. On a slip of paper write out the following charm:

> Gracious, kind and sharp of mind
> Success in my job interview I find.

Put this paper beneath the crystal and memorize the words, so that you can mentally affirm them on the way to the interview and while waiting to be called in. This will keep your mind active and your emotions positive. Leave all the items in place overnight to charge on the pentacle.

The following day, as you get ready, put on the lipstick or tie and see yourself conducting a great interview and coming across well to your prospective employers. Finally, put the slip of paper and the crystal in your pocket or purse, to carry the magic with you. If you get the job, burn the paper and give thanks. If you are unlucky, keep the spell in place on the pentacle and use it for future interviews as there is probably something better coming along you haven't seen yet.

SPELL TO COPE WITH DIFFICULT COLLEAGUES

Items required: An amethyst crystal or amethyst jewellery, a bottle of spring water

Timing: On the waning moon and then whenever you have to work with a difficult colleague, daily if needed

No matter how kind and patient you are, there will be times when a colleague gets on your nerves. Whatever the issue, use this simple spell to absorb their negative energy before it can bring you down. Take the amethyst crystal and let it sit in the light of the waning moon. You can also use a power bracelet of amethyst beads. Allow it to charge until the moon is dark, then take the crystals to work with you and place them between you and the difficult colleague, or keep them on your person, to absorb any negative energy coming your way. If a crystal is too obviously out of place on your desk, use the bottled water for the same purpose — pour a cup of water and place it between you and the person you find challenging. The water will help to absorb their negative energy. Just make sure that you don't drink it! Pour it away or cleanse the crystal under running water at the end of each working day.

SPELL TO SWEETEN UP
A DIFFICULT BOSS

Items required: A small spell jar and stopper, a slip of paper and pen, sugar

Timing: At the new moon

Putting someone's name in the sugar is a traditional folk spell used to bring out their sweeter nature. If you have to work with a difficult boss, it can be hard to stand up for yourself. Bear in mind that things like sexual harassment and workplace bullying should always be reported to your line manager or above. If your boss is simply grumpy, irritable or impatient, however, then try this spell to sweeten them up. Write their name on a slip of paper, roll it up and place it in the spell jar, then fill the jar with sugar. Put on the stopper and keep the jar safe at home, where it will not be found by nosy colleagues!

CHANT FOR A QUIET DAY AT WORK

Items required: None

Timing: When you first get in to work and mentally throughout the day

Sometimes we all need a more relaxed day at work when the phones are quiet, there are no emergencies to see to and the office is calm. This is a little affirmation chant that I have used successfully in many different roles. It shouldn't be used too often, but every now and then it can bring about a much calmer working day and maybe even an early finish. When you first get to work, sit in the car or find a quiet space and repeat the affirmation several times, either out loud or in your head, then repeat as you will, throughout the day.

Bar the door, stop the phone
Bend the time, early home
Quiet office, calm in mind
A peaceful day at work is mine.

SPELL FOR A PAY RISE OR PROMOTION

Items required: An envelope, a green pen, three leaves of fresh mint, a spring of rosemary, three heads of lavender flower, three silver coins, an aventurine crystal, a lock of your hair

Timing: At the new moon

Bear in mind that higher pay or a promotion generally comes with greater responsibility, so be certain this is what you want before you cast this spell. To bring about a pay rise, a promotion or both, take the envelope and write down the new job title and salary you are aiming for inside the flap, using the green pen. Next fill the envelope with the following items: aventurine and mint for prosperity, lavender for luck, rosemary for growth and success, and three silver coins to increase your earnings. Add the tag-lock of your hair, seal the envelope and say:

> Time to shine and room to grow
> Greater success I wish to know
> A promotion sealed within this place
> It comes to me through time and space
> By earth, moon and sun
> By magic it is done.

Once you have been granted the pay rise or promotion, empty the contents of the envelope into the earth, keeping the coins back for future prosperity spells. Give thanks for the new role by burning incense and dedicating it to your chosen deity.

SPELL FOR A SUCCESSFUL BUSINESS VENTURE

Items required: A green candle and holder, a few sunflower seeds, the name of your business or creative venture written down

Timing: During a waxing moon

Lots of people like to have a sideline business alongside their main job. Not only can this provide an additional income stream, it can also offer stress relief from your normal job, giving you something else to focus on. Developing a side business has never been easier, thanks to the internet, and you can set up shop online with relatively few expenses. All you need to do is work out what kind of side-line business you want to create. Once you have this in mind, write it down and place the paper beneath a green candle. Light the candle and place two or three sunflower seeds around the candle holder, to signify the growth of your business venture. Light the candle and say:

> With this light I find my way
> To make my passion bear fruit
> I start this venture from today
> And for the stars I'll shoot!

Allow the candle to burn down naturally and then plant the sunflower seeds in the earth. These are the seeds of your dreams, so tend to them carefully as you set about making your business idea a reality. Good luck!

SPELL TO KEEP MONEY FLOWING INTO YOUR BUSINESS

Items required: Three dried bay leaves, patchouli oil

Timing: On the full moon

To keep the finances of your business venture ticking over, anoint three dried bay leaves with a dab of patchouli oil — both bay and patchouli attract victory and abundance. Place the leaves in the cash register of your business, or wherever you keep all your business finances, say a cash box or a safe. If all your business dealings are online, keep the leaves under your computer to attract more business and financial success your way. Eventually, your sideline business could become your main job, so keep working at it.

CHAPTER EIGHT

Casting for Love and Romance

Witches are often asked to perform magic on behalf of other people, with prosperity magic and love spells being the most frequently requested. While it is possible for a witch to cast a spell for you, it will never be as effective as the spells that you cast for yourself. This is because the witch simply does not have the same emotional investment in the outcome that you do and we mentioned earlier how crucial your emotions are to effective casting. This is especially true when it comes to love spells.

The image of a witch casting spells to *make* someone love them, however, is exaggerated to say the least. You cannot force someone to love you. Either they do or they don't. Maybe they did once, but not any more. They have the free will to choose to love you or to pass you by and that is their prerogative. Love is a gift that must be offered freely and unconditionally. It is not something that can be bartered for. While not everyone is lucky enough to spend their lives billing and cooing at their ideal partner like a pair of doves, there are ways to keep the romance alive for the long term. It all begins, however, with love for yourself.

Self-Love is Key

We live in a world where comparison is rife in society. Social media means that we are constantly bombarded with images of other people, their lifestyle, their clothes, even the food they eat and the places they go. All of this can have a negative impact on your self-esteem if you let it. Remember that social media is a highlight reel and the people you follow will have dark days and low moods, just as you do. After all, nobody's life is perfect.

The impact of all this comparison, however, is that people often find it challenging to love themselves or to think of themselves as worthy human beings. Instead, they fall into the trap of feeling as if they aren't good enough, rich enough, pretty enough or *anything* enough for the modern world. But for someone else to love you, you have to love yourself first. Why is this? Well, it's because bolstering someone else's self-esteem can be exhausting and it is quite a turn-off. People are reluctant to attach themselves to someone who is extremely needy, clingy and dependent on them for feelings of worthiness. They are more likely to be charmed by someone who is in a good place mentally and who is okay with being alone from time to time. So your best chance at a love match is to learn to love yourself first and foremost and to know that you are a worthy human being.

BLESSING FOR SELF-LOVE

Items required: A pink candle and holder, a pink ribbon, a ring that is special to you

Timing: At the time of the new moon to bring out your self-worth

When the first sliver of a new moon is visible in the sky, go to a quiet place, taking the necessary items with you. Light the pink candle and focus on the flame. Then thread the ring onto the pink ribbon and begin to twirl it around the candle flame in a clockwise direction, following the path of the sun. As you do so, chant the words:

I am worthy of love, from myself and others.

Continue for as long as you feel comfortable, then blow out the candle. Repeat each night until the moon is full or the candle has burnt away.

SILENT RITUAL CHARM FOR SELF-LOVE

Items required: A small spell jar and stopper, rose incense stick and holder, a small slip of paper and a pen, a lock of your hair, three rose quartz shards, three dried rose petals, pink Himalayan salt, a pink candle or sealing wax, a pentacle

Timing: At the time of the full moon

To begin with, cleanse the spell jar using the smoke from the rose incense stick, then place the incense in a holder to burn throughout the ritual. Write your name and date of birth on the slip of paper, roll it around the lock of hair and put it into the spell jar. Add the three rose petals and rose quartz shards. Fill the jar with the pink salt, put on the stopper and seal it with pink wax. Leave the spell jar in place on the pentacle until the following full moon, then place it by your bed or on your dressing table to exude its magic.

PINK SELF-LOVE BATH POTION

Items required: Pink candles, pink Himalayan salt, a few rose petals

Timing: Whenever you are feeling frazzled

There will be days when you feel that you cannot do anything right, when you've been running late since the beginning and one mishap led straight into another, leaving you feeling stressed and decidedly frazzled. On those days, show yourself some love with this bath potion. Mix together equal parts pink Himalayan salt and rose petals, then stir this mixture into a hot bath. The salt is known to reduce fatigue, replacing tiredness with feelings of contentment and emotional balance, while the rose petals will soften the skin as the fragrance uplifts you. Wallow in the water for as long as you comfortably can, then dry off and allow your troubles to go down the drain, ensuring that you dispose of the rose petals on the compost heap. Enhance this ritual by using rose-scented toiletries.

Attracting Love

Self-love also involves making the best of your appearance, which in turn helps you to attract a mate. There is no use complaining that you never get invited on a date if you go about your day looking as if you have just been dragged through a hedge. You don't need film-star looks — you just don't want the urge to jump *back* into the hedge because your Mx Wonderful is across the street and you look a mess — what a wasted opportunity for romance that would be! If you want to attract love, prepare for each day as if you are going to meet it head on. Then cast the following spells to enhance your allure and attract a new love interest.

THREE-MOONS SPELL TO ATTRACT LOVE

Items required: Three red candles, half a teaspoon of blessing seeds, mortar and pestle, kitchen roll, rose or lavender oil, an athame or carving tool, a cauldron or heat-proof bowl, a lighter

Timing: On the full moon, three months in a row

Take one of the candles and carve what you are hoping to attract into the length of the wax; you could carve "Love", "Romance" or "New

Boyfriend/Girlfriend". Put half a teaspoon of blessing seeds, also known as nigella seeds, into the mortar and grind to a powder with the pestle. Empty the powder onto a sheet of kitchen roll, anoint the candle in the oil then roll it through the blessing-seed powder, pulling the candle towards you to draw love into your life as you say:

A lover comes by candle's glow
From where or when I do not know
They come to me, true love to share
As the smokes curls through the air
As this wax melts, so do our hearts
Together a new life we start
And by the burning of this flame
Within three/two/one moons I will know their name
So mote it be.

Melt the bottom of the candle and set it in the cauldron. Light the wick and allow it to burn down completely. Repeat with the next candle on the next full moon, adapting the final line of the incantation so that you are counting down the moons until your lover appears.

LOVE WITCH SPELL

Items required: A king or queen of hearts playing card, rose oil or water, a magnet

Timing: On the new moon

If you want to draw more love into your life, then use this spell to become a love magnet! On the night of the new moon, take the items to a quiet place where you will not be disturbed. Take the playing card and anoint the four corners, back and front, with rose oil or rose water, then gently brush the magnet across the image of the king or queen, beginning at the crown and moving down towards the chest of the image. As you do so, chant the words:

Like the king/queen of hearts, I am a magnet to love.

Continue until you feel the magic *pop*, then place the playing card in your purse or wallet and carry it with you at all times. You should notice that you attract more romantic attention in the coming weeks and months.

SILENT CHARM FOR LUCK IN LOVE

Items required: Red or pink sealing wax, greaseproof paper, ground cinnamon powder, a seal which represents love – a heart, rose or cupid design – or a carving tool

Heat the sealing wax and pour or drip it into a large pool on the grease-proof paper, add a sprinkling of cinnamon to draw good luck and blessings towards you, then apply the seal to the cooling wax to create an image. If you do not have a romantic seal, then use your carving tool once the wax has cooled and carve a love heart into the wax. Once the wax has hardened, peel off the greaseproof paper and carry the charm with you to attract lucky love prospects.

WHITE ROSE SPELL TO DETERMINE SOMEONE'S TRUE INTENTIONS

Items required: A single white rose, a white ribbon, a bud vase and water, a slip of paper, a red pen

Timing: At the new moon

Not everyone who flirts with you will have positive or good intentions. The white rose is a symbol of purity and can be used to determine if your lover's intentions towards you are honourable or not. To begin with, write their name on the slip of paper in red ink. Use the ribbon to tie the name tag on to the stem of the rose. Hold your hands over the rose and say:

> A nagging doubt is in my mind so I must test their will
> Their true intentions I would find, be they good or ill
> Rose of love and purity, now tell all with your charm
> Is this lover true to me, or do they mean me harm?

Place the rose in a bud vase of water and care for it well. If it blooms and opens wide, your lover's intentions towards you are pure and kind. If, however, the rose fails to open fully, then wilts and dies, they are holding secrets from you and their intentions are questionable. Let the rose be your guide.

SPELL TO BRING LOVE TO YOUR DOOR

Items required: Three red or pink roses

Timing: Best performed at sunset, during a waxing moon

Pull the petals from three red or pink roses and put them in a pocket, pouch or bowl. Go outside and walk away from your house, enjoying the sunset and imagining sharing the view with a lover. Once you are some way from your home, turn around and begin to walk back. Chant the following words, out loud or in your head:

> Love will come knocking and I will answer.

As you walk, scatter the rose petals so that they form a trail right up to your door, but do not use them all up. Keep a few back and place these in a pouch or trinket dish by your bed. Love should come knocking within a full lunar phase.

APPLE SPELL TO DEEPEN BONDS OF LOVE

Items required: At least one apple (more if you choose the pie option), a sharp knife, cinnamon and nutmeg

Timing: Best performed during a waxing moon, or on a special anniversary

Tradition states that to share an apple with your partner will help to deepen the bonds of love between you, and there are two ways that you can use this magic. For a simple charm, cut an apple in half horizontally through the core to expose the seed pentacle in the middle, sprinkle it with cinnamon and nutmeg for a fruitful union, then give one half to your lover and eat the other half yourself. Alternatively, you can choose to bake the magic into an apple pie, by following a basic recipe and adding a generous sprinkling of the spices to the apples just before you cover them in pastry. For added magic, top the pie with the initials of you and your lover in pastry, then share the pie as part of a romantic dinner.

SILENT SEED SPELL TO CHOOSE BETWEEN SUITORS

Items required: A pink, white or cream pillar candle, three (or however many suitors you have) pumpkin seeds, a black felt-tip pen, a lighter

Timing: On the full to waning moon to whittle down the competition

If you are a flower to bees (lucky you!) and you are having difficulty in choosing between suitors, then use this simple spell. First write the initial of each suitor on one of the pumpkin seeds with black pen. Next heat up the side of the candle with the lighter so that you can stick the seeds to the candle. Make sure that all the seeds are in a row, at the same height. Each suitor is now represented with a seed that bears his or her initial. Finally, light the wick of the candle. As the candle burns, the seeds should fall, but the seed which sticks the longest is the suitor you should choose as they are the type to stick around.

SPELL TO HEAL A RIFT BETWEEN LOVERS

Items required: An empty jar and lid, a jar of runny honey, pink paper, scissors, a pen, pink or red sealing wax

Timing: During the waning moon to remove the discord between you

Relationships can be hard work at times and you won't always see eye to eye with your partner. If an argument has left a lingering atmosphere of discord between you, cast this spell to help heal the rift. Cut two love hearts from the pink paper. Write your name on one heart and your lover's name on the other. Hold your hands over the hearts and visualize the rift healing. Imagine enjoying happy, romantic times with your partner again. Drop both hearts into the empty jar, then add enough runny honey to cover them, surrounding the couple in sweetness as you say:

> I am sweet to you, you are sweet to me
> Together we restore harmony
> Heart to heart our spirits lift
> By sweetest spell we heal this rift.

Seal the spell jar with the sealing wax and keep it in the bedroom. Remember to let bygones be bygones and know that to move forward, you must let go of the past.

TWO-HEARTS SPELL FOR LONG-DISTANCE LOVE

Items required: Two heart-shaped pebbles, stones or crystals, a pentacle, a chalice of wine or juice

Timing: Each full moon to keep the bond strong while apart

How do you ensure that your long-distance love survives? Well, you need to find things that forge a bond across the distance, things that you can both appreciate and which remind you of one another, no matter where you are. The moon is an obvious choice, for its light is reflected the world over. Make a pact with your partner that you will think of each other whenever you see a full moon, and send blessings their way. Then enhance this sentiment by placing the two heart pebbles on the pentacle in the moonlight, toast the moon with the chalice and say:

> I drink to you, my lover true
> No matter where thou be
> I drink to the moon and ask this boon
> To send my lover safe home to me.

Send your love to your partner, using the moon as your messenger, and finish the wine or juice. Leave the two hearts side by side until the moon begins to wane, then repeat the spell each full moon.

When Love Turns Bad

Occasionally a relationship will fade and deteriorate over time. When this happens the pain can be acute as you are forced to say goodbye, not only to your partner but also to the life you lived and the future that you planned together. Like many things in life, love can have a shelf life. People come into our lives for a reason, a season or, if we are very lucky, a lifetime, but there are no guarantees. Even the sweetest love can fade over time, leading to loss and heartbreak. If you are nursing a heartache, use these spells to help you cope.

FLY-BY-NIGHT SPELL

Items required: A notepad and pen, sage essential oil, a cauldron, twigs to make a small fire

Timing: On the waning moon, outdoors

If you have discovered that your lover has deceived you or let you down badly, use this spell to clear them from your life. We think of a fly-by-night as someone who is only around for what they can get and has no real intentions of sticking around for a committed relationship. Perhaps you have learned that they are already married, they are moving away, or something else. Whatever their transgression might be, this spell will help you to clear their energies from your life so that you can move on without them.

First write a letter to your ex-partner explaining how they have made you feel. Tell them of your confusion, resentment and upset. Don't worry, you are never going to send this letter! Just get all your feelings, hurt and anger down on paper. Next make a small fire in the cauldron using the twigs. Anoint the letter with the sage oil to cleanse this fly-by-night individual from your life, then fold the letter into the shape of a paper aeroplane. Hold the plane to your heart and say:

Fly-by-night, leave my sight
Never to return
You had your chance, but by happenstance
The truth I had to learn
The love I felt now must wither
It fades within my heart
You let me down so go from hither
I am glad that you depart!

As you say the last line of the incantation, throw the paper aeroplane into the fire and watch it crash and burn.

SPELL TO HEAL A BROKEN HEART

Items required: A heart-shaped stone or crystal, tissues

Timing: From full to dark moon

If you have had your heart broken, try this little spell to kick-start the healing process. Hold the pebble to your heart as you think about the circumstances of the heartbreak. If tears bubble up, wipe them with a tissue. When you are ready, kiss the stone and wrap it in the tissue as you say:

> I wrap my heart in tears so that I can release the sorrow it holds.

Next go for a walk, taking the stone with you. Try to find a crossroads where three or four paths meet and bury the stone in the earth there. Next say:

> Earth heals my heart which is heavy and sore
> Let healing begin, that it bleeds no more
> Take all my heart's trouble deep into your glen
> Lighten my load, that I might love again.

When the heart is safely buried, walk away from the site and do not look back.

CHAPTER NINE

Casting for Healing and Balance

Healing is not the same as curing. Some illnesses cannot be cured, others are by their very nature a temporary affliction. Healing is about restoring balance in mind, body and spirit. In magic, healing is the process of bringing about a sense of equilibrium and getting things back into kilter. While some healing rituals do work to alleviate the symptoms of illness, others are designed to restore the balance that has been temporarily lost, so a spell to help with symptoms of PMS aims to redress the imbalance brought about through the monthly cycle of hormones — it doesn't *cure* the cycle, it just makes its symptoms easier to bear.

Witchcraft has always been a healing tradition; the wise women of old acted as local doctors and midwives to their neighbours. In the days before antibiotics and vaccinations, people relied heavily on herbal remedies which were their only source of medicine. Being a wise woman during this time could be a dangerous business, however, as many of the plants used medicinally could also have nasty side effects, such as digitalis, or the humble foxglove.

You should never claim to be a medical practitioner or to have healed someone. There are firm laws in place that regulate medicine and medical practice, which mean that unless you are a GP you are not qualified to offer a diagnosis or to claim that you can cure anyone. What you *can* do is cast spells to offer strength and positivity to someone who is going through a tough time and you can use simple alternative practices such as herbal blends, crystal therapy and aromatherapy potions to offer comfort to yourself and others when daily life gets hard. You can also offer the most traditional of healing rituals, tea and sympathy, because you should never underestimate the power of a listening ear to help someone to feel better.

The gentle healing rituals in this chapter make use of easily available herbs, essentials oils and spell ingredients. Use these spells responsibly and always do your own research into any herbs or oils before you use them, particularly if you are substituting ingredients or if you are pregnant or trying to conceive.

Tisanes, Infusions and Simples

Many healing potions come in the form of infusions or tisanes. An infusion is made by steeping leaves in boiling water. When you make a cup of tea you are making an infusion. A tisane is made by steeping other plant ingredients — flowers, roots, shoots and spices — in hot water. Usually, a tisane is a blend of more than one plant, while an infusion is made with a single plant such as tea leaves, and is also known as a *simple*. Most herbal tisanes do not contain caffeine so they are best enjoyed before bed to aid relaxation. Some tisanes can also be used as restorative bath soaks, by adding them to the water as you draw a bath. Lavender and lemon balm, for example, is good for a calming bath, while rose geranium can help to ease menstrual pains.

LEMON AND GINGER POTION TO STRENGTHEN IMMUNITY

Items required: Two lemons, ginger root, approx. two teaspoons honey, 2 litres (3½ pints) spring water

Timing: Make during a new moon

This potion is great for strengthening the immune system and for easing or warding off colds, flus and bad coughs during the winter. Ideally you should drink a hot cup of this tisane every morning, especially during the colder months. Pour the spring water into a pan and add ginger root (vary the quantity according to your preference). Slice the lemons and add those too. Heat the mixture and, once the potion has got hot, add a couple of teaspoons of honey. Simmer for five minutes until the aromas fill the air, then strain, cool and decant into a clean glass bottle. Drink a warm cup of this tisane every day. The mixture should be kept in the fridge and is good for two to three days.

COLTSFOOT AND EUCALYPTUS STEAM BATH

Items required: One teaspoon each of dried coltsfoot and eucalyptus leaves, a large bowl, hot water, a large towel

Timing: Use whenever you have a bad head cold or chesty chough

Steaming the lungs is a traditional way to provide relief from congestion. It is an easy way to treat a bad head cold or a chesty cough, as the steam helps to clear the airways. The herbs in this steam bath are known to break up mucus and ease breathing difficulty. First put the dried leaves into the bottom of the bowl and pour on hot water from the kettle. Place the bowl on a table and sit down. Put the towel over your head and the bowl to create a tent, and inhale the herbal steam. Keep inhaling the steam for about 20 minutes, or until the water has cooled. Repeat twice a day, morning and evening, for the best results. As an alternative, you can add this potion to bath water instead. This is sometimes a better option for small children.

CLOVE OIL FOR TOOTHACHE

Items required: Clove oil or half a clove, a cotton pad

Timing: Use whenever you have a toothache

The nagging pain of a toothache can be most uncomfortable and, while this traditional remedy is no replacement for a visit to the dentist, it should help to make you more comfortable until you get to your dental appointment. Place a few drops of clove oil on a cotton pad and tuck this onto the affected tooth. Alternatively, cut a clove in half and place this by the tooth instead. Needless to say, due to the choking hazard, this remedy isn't suitable for children.

FEVERFEW TO EASE A HEADACHE

Items required: One teaspoon of dried peppermint or feverfew leaves, honey, lavender essential oil

Timing: Use as soon as you feel the first niggle of a headache

Feverfew or peppermint tea is very good for soothing a headache or the beginning of a migraine. However, feverfew should not be used if pregnant or breastfeeding, nor should you use it if you are taking any medication for thinning blood or for blood pressure, so use peppermint instead. Steep the leaves in hot water for 3–4 minutes, strain and sip slowly. Rubbing a drop or two of lavender essential oil into your temples can also help to reduce the headache, as can lying in a darkened room. Try to avoid any kind of stimulant such as caffeine, tobacco or chocolate, which can all exacerbate a headache. Also avoid any screen time, so no TV, laptop, gaming or scrolling through your phone. Turn off all devices and allow the tea and oil time to work, without doing anything to counteract the beneficial effects.

ARNICA TO BRING OUT BRUISING

Items required: An empty dark glass bottle, arnica essential oil, 10ml (¼fl oz) almond oil

Timing: Make up on a waxing moon if possible

Arnica is traditionally used to treat bumps, bruises, sprains and joint pain. It is a natural anti-inflammatory so it can ease lots of mild aches, pains and soreness. Due to its potency, you need to dilute it in a carrier oil first, so add 5 drops of arnica essential oil to 10ml (¼fl oz) of almond oil. Store it in a dark glass bottle, away from sunlight. To ease the pain of bumps and bruises, gently rub a little of the oil on to the affected area. This will help the bruise to bloom quickly and therefore heal more rapidly too. Apply daily until the bruise is gone or the soreness has eased. Do not use arnica on broken skin as it is too strong and can cause irritation.

ROSE-WATER COMPRESS
TO BRING DOWN SWELLING

Items required: A crepe bandage, rose water or rose essential oil, spring water, a bowl

Timing: Use on sprains and swollen joints

Rose is a good all-round plant, which is why it is used in so many beauty products and natural remedies. It makes an excellent base for a cold compress, which can be applied to reduce swelling caused by sprains. Place an unrolled bandage into a large bowl, add cold spring water to completely cover and soak the bandage. Next add two tablespoons of rose water, or 6 drops of rose essential oil. Stir the bandage around in the rose water, then place the bowl and its contents into the fridge for about 10 minutes. Once the bandage has cooled and soaked up the rose water, wring it out and apply the damp bandage to the swollen area, being careful not to wrap the bandage too tightly. If the swelling hasn't reduced with an hour seek medical attention.

CALENDULA TO SOOTHE IRRITATED SKIN

Items required: Two tablespoons of dried calendula flowers, 50ml (1½fl oz) almond or sunflower oil, an empty bottle

Timing: Make at the time of the new moon

Calendula is a little golden marigold flower that is frequently added to beauty products. It is a mild astringent and has anti-fungal properties. It is a gentle way to treat mild skin irritation, mild sunburn, rashes and blemishes. It can also be used as an anti-aging treatment when applied to dark spots to make them appear less visible. To make calendula oil, drop two tablespoons of dried calendula flowers into a bottle and add 50ml (1½fl oz) of a carrier oil such as almond, olive or sunflower. Let the flowers steep in the oil, shaking the bottle each day. There is no need to strain, you can leave the flowers in the oil. Apply the potion to irritated skin to soothe and smooth. Do not use if pregnant as calendula can bring on menstruation.

GERANIUM MASSAGE OIL FOR MENSTRUAL DISCOMFORT

Items required: An empty dark glass bottle, 30ml (1fl oz) almond oil, rose geranium essential oil

Timing: Make on the full moon

This gentle message oil can help to alleviate the discomfort associated with painful periods, such as stomach cramps, lower back pain and breast tenderness. Pour 30ml (1fl oz) of almond oil into a clean dark glass bottle and add 6–10 drops of rose geranium oil. Gently massage the oil into the stomach, lower back and breasts to quickly ease the discomfort. Use every month as soon as you feel the first twinges of menstrual pain.

RASPBERRY AND SAGE FOR SORE THROATS

Items required: Half a teaspoon of dried raspberry leaves, half a teaspoon of dried sage leaves, honey

Timing: Use whenever you have a sore throat

Steep the herbs in boiling water for around five minutes, then strain and add honey to taste. Use this infusion as a gargle to soothe sore throats and tonsillitis.

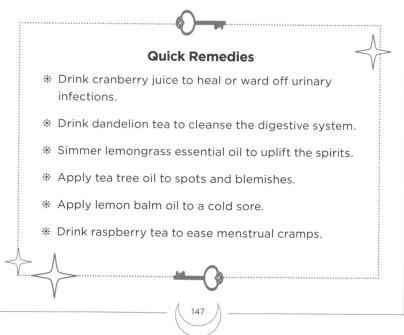

Quick Remedies

* Drink cranberry juice to heal or ward off urinary infections.

* Drink dandelion tea to cleanse the digestive system.

* Simmer lemongrass essential oil to uplift the spirits.

* Apply tea tree oil to spots and blemishes.

* Apply lemon balm oil to a cold sore.

* Drink raspberry tea to ease menstrual cramps.

SPELL TO SEND STRENGTH TO A SICK PERSON

Items required: Three pieces of narrow blue ribbon or cord, a lock of the sick person's hair

Timing: On a full moon

Willow trees are known as wishing trees, because it is said that a wish whispered beneath its boughs is sure to be granted. Trees of all kinds are also a great source of strength. This spell calls on the spirit of the willow tree to lend strength to the person who is ill. To begin with, you will need to ask the patient's permission to work a healing spell on their behalf. Once permission is granted, obtain a lock of their hair and begin to plait the three ribbons together, weaving the lock of hair into the plait about halfway down. Secure the braid and then take it with you to your chosen willow tree. Stand beneath the tree, tie the ribbon to a branch and say:

> Willow tree, wishing tree
> Send your strength to one dear to me
> I tie this braid with hair within
> I ask for strength and swift healing
> Send your blessing to the one
> Who needs it now, so be it done.

Give thanks to the spirit of the tree and walk away when you feel ready, leaving the ribbon in place on the tree.

CHARM TO MAKE A HEALING POPPET

Items required: Blue felt, a needle and thread, a pen and piece of paper, dried herbs for healing – lavender, sage, calendula, camomile and feverfew, a pentacle

Timing: On the full moon

To begin with, write the name of the person you want to send healing energies to on the slip of paper, along with their date of birth. Next fashion a poppet from the felt, cutting two humanoid shapes and stitching them together, but leaving the head open. Place the name tag into the poppet first and say:

(name) I send healing energies your way this day.

Fill the poppet with equal amounts of the dried herbs and stitch up the head, then say:

Little poppet I fashioned you from love
I name you for _____
May their illness fade way, may their recovery be swift
May healing magic pass from you to them, this charm is your gift
When this work is complete and all is said and done
I'll cast your herbs onto the earth to once more feel the sun.

Keep the poppet in a safe place. Once the illness has passed, unstitch it and scatter the herbs on the earth. Burn the name tag and the felt poppet, giving thanks.

A CANDLE RITUAL FOR HEALING

Items required: A blue candle and holder, lavender oil, an athame or carving tool, a photograph of the person you have permission to cast for

Timing: Waxing moon

To begin, place the photograph where you can see it as you work. This will be your focus as you cast the spell. Next carve the name of the person you are sending healing energies to, down the length of the candle. Anoint the candle with lavender oil, from the top to the middle and them from the bottom to the middle. This will help to draw healing energies to them from all sides. Set the anointed candle in a holder and light it. Close your eyes and picture the sick person in your mind. Imagine that they are surrounded by a sphere of healing blue light. As you visualize this, begin to chant the following words:

Healed from above, healed from below
Healed from all sides, good health you now know
Healed from without, healed from within
Healed in all ways, let the healing begin.

Continue this chant for as long as you can — you can chant in your head if you want to. Place the candle next to the photograph, so that its light shines on their face. Let the candle burn down naturally and know that you have sent good energies to your loved one in their hour of need.

VALLEY OF THE SHADOW RITUAL

Items required: Small black candle, myrrh essential oil (or frankincense or sandalwood oils)

Timing: On a waning to dark moon

Sometimes all the healing spells in the world won't change the outcome, and if someone has been diagnosed with a terminal illness then it is cruel and irresponsible to offer false hope. It is one of the hardest things in the world to cope with when you know for a fact that someone you love is dying and there is nothing you can do to prevent it. Even medical science has its limits, so you should not feel bad that your magic cannot work miracles. You might not be able to offer a cure, but you can perform rituals to help smooth out the dark path you and your loved one must take, in order to make the journey as gentle as possible for both of you. This ritual is designed to be repeated whenever you have need of it, but is best performed on a waning moon. Take the black candle and anoint it with essential oil of myrrh. If you can't find myrrh you can use sandalwood or frankincense oil as a substitute. Anoint the whole candle from top to bottom, then place it in a holder and light the wick as you say:

I'll walk the shadow-way with you
I see all that you're going through
I'll hold your hand till it be time
I'm safe in your heart, you're safe in mine
Through all the dark days and nights ahead
My spirit is there, beside your bed
I'll walk with you till we must part
Spirit to spirit and heart to heart
Blessed be.

SPELL TO INVOKE
A HEALING ANGEL

Items required: An angel lapel pin, a pentacle, a tea-light and holder

Timing: Whenever you need a little extra healing power

Angels are universally recognized as benevolent guardians and guides. They can assist with all manner of things, but you must ask for their help before they can intervene. If someone you know needs a little extra healing, then invoking an angel is a good way to ensure that they are comforted, supported and guided as they navigate their way through illness or trauma. For this ritual you will need a little angel lapel pin, which you can purchase from most gift shops or online. You are going to give this pin to the person who needs extra healing, but first you need to empower it to its purpose and invoke angelic energies to go with it. Place the pin in the centre of the pentacle to charge. Light the tea-light and call on celestial help with the following invocation:

Angels of healing from far and wide
I invoke your assistance, be by my side
I cast forth this spell to help heal one I love
I ask for your aid, shine your light from above
Let your magic be felt through the charm of this pin
And as you hold (name) in your wings, let the healing begin
So mote it be.

Leave the pin in place to keep charging for 24 hours and allow the candle to burn out. The next time you see your loved one, give them the pin and tell them it is a reminder that they can all on their angels for help when they need to.

Conclusion

AND THE SPELL IS CAST

I hope that you have enjoyed reading this Book of Shadows and Spells and that you have begun to practise some of the practical magic within its pages. Magic is a natural aspect of life for lots of people and I trust that you will come to reach for this grimoire time and time again, whenever you need to. My aim has been to show you how simple and accessible magic really is, for those who are brave enough to try it.

You now have at your fingertips all the information you need to live a charmed life, and while some of these spells might appear simple, I encourage you to try them nonetheless, bearing in mind that simplicity is a power in and of itself. This book is designed to be a jumping-off point too – something you can be inspired by when it comes to devising your own spells, rituals and blessings.

Of all the many enchantments in this book, I hope that you have found something that has proved useful to you and which has made you feel stronger and more powerful than before, whether that is a piece of psychological information you needed to read or a particular spell you needed to cast. Many of the charms and enchantments here are ones that I have used repeatedly in my own life, while some I have devised specifically for this collection. Keep this Book of Shadows close to your heart and it will serve you well. Be bold in your magic and when life grows dark, reach for these shadows; when you need more light, call on these shadows and when all is well, celebrate with these blessed shadows. Farewell, my magical reader, until our paths cross again for our next merry meeting. Live magically!

Serene blessings,
Marie Bruce x

Index